CORN / MAÍZ

Doreen Gonzales
Traducción al español: Ma. Pilar Sanz

PowerKiDS press. & **Editorial Buenas Letras**™
New York

Published in 2009 by The Rosen Publishing Group, Inc.
29 East 21st Street, New York, NY 10010

First Edition

Editor: Amelie von Zumbusch
Book Design: Kate Laczynski
Photo Researcher: Jessica Gerweck

Photo Credits: Cover, p. 1 © Bruce Dale/Getty Images; cover texture, p. 1 © www.istockphoto.com/Walter Fumagalli; p. 4 © www.istockphoto.com; pp. 7, 15, 19, 20 Shutterstock.com; p. 8 © Dea/G. Dagli Orti/Getty Images; pp. 11, 12 © Superstock.com; p. 16 © Carl Tremblay/Getty Images.

Library of Congress Cataloging-in-Publication Data

Gonzales, Doreen.
    Corn = Maíz / Doreen Gonzales ; traducción al español Ma. Pilar Sanz. — 1. ed.
        p. cm. — (Native foods of Latin America)
English text, parallel Spanish translation.
Includes index.
ISBN 978-1-4358-2723-3 (library binding)
1. Corn—Juvenile literature. I. Sanz, Ma. Pilar (María Pilar) II. Title. III. Title: Maíz. IV. Series.
SB191.M2G612 2009
641.3'315098—dc22
                        2008020807

Manufactured in the United States of America

CONTENTS

CONTENIDO

People all around the world eat corn. Corn first came from Mexico. It has been an important food in Latin America for many years. Sometimes, Latin Americans eat **roasted** corn. Other dishes are made from ground corn.

En todo el mundo la gente come maíz. El maíz viene de México, y durante muchos años ha sido un alimento muy importante en Latinoamérica. En Latinoamérica se come el maíz **asado**. Otras comidas se hacen con maíz molido.

The first people to grow corn were Native Americans living in Mexico about 6,000 years ago. The Indians planted seeds from wild corn. They learned how to grow bigger corn and how to store corn for winter. This knowledge quickly spread across Mexico and Central America.

Los indígenas de México fueron los primeros en cultivar el maíz, hace unos 6,000 años. Al principio, sembraron las semillas de maíz silvestre. Con el tiempo aprendieron a cultivar el maíz y a conservarlo durante el invierno. Este conocimento se expandió rápidamente por México y América Central.

7

Corn became the main food of many Indians. A group of Native Americans called the Mayas even believed people were created from corn. Some Native Americans ground corn into cornmeal. Indians called the Aztecs used cornmeal to make flat bread called *tlaxcallis*.

El maíz se convirtió en el alimento principal de muchos pueblos indígenas como los mayas y los aztecas. Los mayas incluso creían que los seres humanos habían sido creados del maíz. Algunos pueblos indígenas hacían harina con el maíz. Los aztecas usaban esta harina para hacer un tipo de pan llamado *tlaxcalli*.

In the 1400s, Spanish **explorers** reached Latin America. The Spanish took corn back to Europe with them. Latin Americans started using foods the Spanish brought, such as cheese, in their cooking. Tlaxcallis became known by the Spanish name *tortillas*.

En los años 1400, **exploradores** españoles llegaron a lo que hoy es Latinoamérica. Los españoles llevaron el maíz a Europa. Por su parte, los indígenas comenzaron a usar algunos alimentos que habían traído los españoles, como el queso. Las *tlaxcallis* se dieron a conocer con el nombre de tortillas.

Today, many Latin Americans still eat tortillas every day. They use them in many dishes, like tacos and quesadillas. Tamales are another common food using corn. A tamale is made from corn **dough** that is filled with meat, cheese, or vegetables and steamed in a corn **husk**.

Hoy, muchos latinoamericanos continúan comiendo tortillas todos los días, en platillos como tacos o quesadillas. Los tamales son otro alimento en el que se usa maíz. Un tamal se hace con **masa** de maíz rellena con carne, queso o verduras. Los tamales se envuelven en hojas de maíz y se cocinan al vapor.

Many Latin American countries have their own special corn dishes. In Peru, children love *chicha morada*, a sweet corn drink that is often made with cinnamon. *Pupusas* are common in El Salvador. These thick tortillas are stuffed with cheese, vegetables, or meat.

Muchos países de Latinoamérica tienen sus propias especialidades de maíz. En Perú, a los niños les encanta beber chicha morada, una bebida de maíz y canela. En El Salvador, son muy famosas las pupusas. Estas gruesas tortillas se rellenan de queso, verduras o carne.

16

Soon after corn arrived in Europe, it spread to other parts of the world. Many countries have special corn dishes. *Kpekple* is a cornmeal and fish stew common in Ghana. In the United States, foods such as grits, johnnycakes, and cornbread are made from corn.

Cuando el maíz llegó a Europa, no tardó mucho en expandirse al resto del mundo. Muchos países tienen platillos especiales con maíz. En Ghana el *kpekpe*, un guisado de harina de maíz y pescado, es muy popular. En los Estados Unidos, alimentos como el pan de maíz, los *grits*, y los *johnnycakes* se hacen usando maíz.

People grow corn all around the world. Corn grows on tall, leafy **stalks**. The plant's tassel, or flower, grows from the top. Ears form on the stalks. Each ear has many seeds, or kernels, covered by a husk of leaves.

El maíz se siembra en todo el mundo. El maíz crece en largos **tallos** con espigas, o flores, en la parte de arriba. Cada espiga tiene muchas semillas, o granos de maíz, y está cubierta de hojas.

19

There are many kinds of corn. Some kinds of corn grow well in wet places. Others grow best where it is dry. Corn kernels can be white, yellow, orange, red, blue, or purple. Sometimes, corn has several colors on the same ear.

Hay muchos tipos de maíz. Algunos crecen en lugares húmedos. Otros, crecen mejor en tierras secas. Los granos de maíz pueden ser de color blanco, amarillo, anaranjado, rojo, azul o violeta. En ocasiones, una misma mazorca tiene muchos colores distintos.

Today, corn is used for more things than just eating. Sweeteners made from corn are put into soda and other drinks. Corn is fed to cows and pigs. Scientists make **medicines**, plastics, and even **fuels** from corn!

Actualmente, el maíz se usa en muchos artículos. Edulcorantes, o sustancias endulzantes, hechos con maíz se usan en sodas y otras bebidas. Las vacas y los puercos se alimentan con maíz. ¡Los científicos usan maíz para hacer **medicinas**, plásticos y hasta **combustible**!

GLOSSARY

dough (DOH) A thick mix from which food is made.

explorers (ek-SPLOR-erz) People who travel and look for new land.

fuels (FYOOLZ) Things used to make warmth or power.

husk (HUSK) The dry covering of a fruit, plant, or seed.

medicines (MEH-duh-sinz) Drugs that a doctor gives you to help fight illness.

roasted (ROHST-ed) Cooked over high heat or in an oven.

stalks (STOKS) Thin parts of plants that hold up other parts.

GLOSARIO

asar Cocinar en altas temperaturas en una parrilla o en el horno.

combustibles (los) Materiales usados para crear energía.

exploradores (los) Personas que viajan en busca de tierras desconocidas.

masa (la) Mezcla que se usa para preparar tortillas, pan y pasteles.

medicinas (las) Drogas que recetan los doctores para curar una enfermedad.

tallo (el) Eje de la planta que sostiene las hojas.

INDEX

A
Aztecs, 9

D
dough, 13

E
El Salvador, 14

F
fuel, 22

H
husk, 13, 18

K
kernels, 18
kpekple, 17

M
Mayas, 9
medicine, 22
Mexico, 5–6

P
Peru, 14
plastic, 22

S
seeds, 6

sweetener, 22

T
tamale, 13
tassel, 18
tlaxcallis, 9, 10
tortillas, 10, 14

U
United States, 17

ÍNDICE

A
aztecas, 9

C
combustible, 22

E
El Salvador, 14
endulzantes, 22
espigas, 18

Estados Unidos, 17

G
granos, 18

K
kpekple, 17

M
masa, 13
mayas, 9
medicina, 22
México, 5–6

P
Perú, 14
plástico, 22

S
semillas, 6

T
tamal, 13
tlaxcallis, 9, 10
tortillas, 10, 14

WEB SITES / PÁGINAS DE INTERNET

Due to the changing nature of Internet links, PowerKids Press and Editorial Buenas Letras have developed an online list of Web sites related to the subject of this book. This site is updated regularly. Please use this link to access the list: www.powerkidslinks.com/nfla/corn/